little book

BIG PLANTS

bring the outside in with
over 45 friendly giants

emma sibley

photography by adam laycock

Hardie Grant

QUADRILLE

CONTENTS

I would love to dedicate this book to my grandparents, Ben and Ethel Howard, for passing on their green fingers to me.

INTRODUCTION

BIG PLANTS FOR THE HOME

———

When I see a large, handsome house plant, I often wonder about the journey it has taken to reach that size. Has it been nurtured lovingly by one owner, swapped as part of a house plant enthusiasts' group, or passed down from a family member, with propagations given away and shared with relatives and friends?

Whether you prefer to buy a young plant so that you can watch it grow and flourish or you are all about the instant gratification of bringing home a large, ready-formed specimen, there is one thing you can almost always guarantee – your plant will continue to grow and adapt to fill your space.

This book explains how to nurture and care for these large plants. It will take you through over 45 different house plants as well as featuring interviews with house plant aficionados about their favourite giants.

HOW TO USE THIS BOOK

Each entry includes key information about caring for that particular plant. All the information is clearly organised under appropriate symbols which will help you give your plants everything they need to grow and thrive.

KEY TO SYMBOLS

LIGHT

HEIGHT

TOXICITY

WATER

FEED

AIR PURIFIER

MISTING

Each plant is given its common and Latin names; occasionally these are the same. The Latin or botanical name provides information about the relationship between plants and is known as the taxonomic status. All plants belong to a particular family and these are divided into *genera* (the plural of *genus*). The Latin name of each plant consists of two words: the *genus* and the species. The *genus* is a collective name for a group of plants, and the species (or specific epithet) tells you more about a particular plant.

BASIC PLANT CARE

House plants have three basic requirements: light, water and soil. Provide them with the right conditions, and you will have happy, healthy plants.

LIGHT LEVELS
The lighting advice in this book is just a guideline. If your plant is not looking happy, experiment with different positions.

BRIGHT LIGHT
This is also referred to as direct sunlight (Sun). A west- or south-facing window will provide bright light, which means receiving 5 to 6 hours of direct sunlight a day.

BRIGHT, INDIRECT LIGHT
This is also referred to as bright, indirect sunlight (BIDL). The windowsill of an east-facing window, or a plant set back about 60cm (2ft) or so from a west- or south-facing window will provide bright, indirect light. This ensures that the plant is not exposed to direct sunlight, but it is receiving plenty of light. If you'd like your plant to sit on the sill of a west- or south-facing window, introduce a sheer curtain or sun shade.

LOW LIGHT

A north-facing window provides low light, or any room that is obviously in shade (from other buildings or trees) and doesn't get any direct sunlight during the day.

WATERING

As with light levels, the watering information given with each plant entry is only a guideline. For most house plants, the soil should dry out slightly between watering. The exceptions are those plants that either like a very wet or a very dry soil. To test, dip your finger 2.5cm (1in) or so in the compost and if it's dry, give the plant a water with tepid water. If not, wait a few days and try again. Most house plants need good drainage and hate standing in water. Ensure that the actual plant pot has drainage holes in the base, and that the soil is free-draining (see below). Don't let the plant sit in a saucer or pot of water. If the plant is too heavy to lift in order to drain away excess water from its saucer, use a sponge to draw the water away.

SOIL AND FEEDING

It's advisable to use a dedicated house plant compost for indoor plants, which is designed to give your plants the right medium to grow and flourish. If you feel the soil needs to be more free-draining, add a handful of horticultural sand or grit to the mix. To feed your plants, use a liquid house plant feed diluted in water, following the manufacturer's instructions. Always add feed to damp soil, never to dry as this could burn the roots.

CHOOSING A PLANT

One of the key decisions you need to make when buying a plant is whether you want a small one that has the potential to grow into a big house plant or whether you would prefer to start with a plant that's already an adequate size. Not all plants will grow into a big room filler. Some plants, such as the *Monstera delicosa*, have leaves that increase in size as the whole plant develops. Compare this to its sister, the *Monstera adansonii*, which will grow to take up more space but its leaves will pretty much stay the same size. Most garden centres and plant nurseries will stock younger and smaller specimens of the plants mentioned in this book, which will allow you to move and train them to adapt to your home as they grow. When investing in a larger plant, you will need to know where you are going to place it so that there will be enough room for you both to live in harmony together! (See the Living with Big Plants section on page 13.)

LIVING WITH BIG PLANTS

It's all well and good wanting large plants, but you need to be able to live with them and provide them with the space to move and grow without being damaged or unsettled. However, with some forethought even a small apartment can accommodate at least one statement plant.

Look out for suitable spots. This could be a corner, next to the sofa - a tall Kentia Palm would be very at home here, especially if it is a darkish location. A small space on a shelf is the perfect perch for a long String of Hearts or a Hoya. The beauty of this position is that as the plants grow you can continue to move them up the shelves. Similarly, you can find some beautiful indoor wall-mounted plant pots these days that create a feature on a bare wall. Use them instead of a framed print, or place alongside one.

Indoor plant clips are also a genius way of training a vine, such as Devil's Ivy, to climb up a wall to form a living backdrop as opposed to hanging it from a pot or clambering up a moss stick. Hide the plant pot behind a sofa or beside a chest of drawers to save on space.

Hanging plants are also perfect for saving on floor space. Most of the ones that you can buy, such as String of Hearts or Devil's Ivy, will come with a basic plastic ceiling hook, but these are super easy to pop off and replace with a macramé plant hanger and bright ceramic pot to match your interior.

FROM SMALL TO BIG

All house plants grow at different rates. The position in which you place your plant - how much light and heat it gets - will affect its growth. For example, the exact same plant may grow far quicker in your bright, south-facing front room than one placed in your best friend's dark hallway. You just need to work with the conditions that you have. Plants will also grow at a much greater rate over the summer months, putting on a massive growth spurt between April and September, then slowing down over the winter months when many plants go into dormancy.

Not every home is blessed with sunny, well-lit rooms. Where light levels are low, few house plants will be able to thrive and grow unaided. This is where grow lights for indoor growing can come in handy. These specialist lights are designed to give plants an extra boost of light that they can convert into energy. A high-quality horticultural **LED** lamp should be sufficient for your basic house plants. Put it on a timer for about 8-12 hours during the day so that your plants can also have their natural rest period at night. If you are unsure about which light to get, consult an expert to get the right lamp for your space.

CREATING THE ILLUSION OF A BIGGER PLANT

─────

So you have bought a plant, placed it at home in the spot you had in mind, but the result is a bit underwhelming. What to do? The solution is planters that can instantly make your house plants grow without the wait!

RAISED PLANTERS

You can find some really cool raised planters nowadays to add extra height. Your local garden centre is a good source, but also try high-street interior stores as well. A single raised planter or a group of them can create instant impact if hidden next to a sofa or a chest of drawers. You can also use upturned baskets or small side tables to create the same effect.

PLANTERS FOR MULTIPLE PLANTS

These are a great way to fill a space without having to buy a massive plant. Choose a planter that has sufficient diameter to accommodate two or three plants of the same variety. False Shamrock, Prayer Plants and ferns work really well planted in this way. You will also often see larger Rubber Plants and Umbrella Plants for sale with two or three stems to a pot, giving the illusion of one very full plant rather than many little ones. *Monstera adansonii* looks amazing planted two, three or even four to a wide, round planter, an eye-catching centerpiece for a dining or coffee table.

REPOTTING LARGER PLANTS

Actively growing house plants will need to be repotted every year or so. There are two clear signs that a plant needs repotting: it's stopped growing because it's used up all of the nutrients in its current compost, or its roots are forcing their way out of the base of its pot, asking to go up a container size. However, as plants reach maturity they will need to be repotted less and less, and to be honest this is great news as the bigger they get, the heavier and harder this becomes!

If you are dealing with a particularly big plant, such as a giant Fiddle Leaf Fig, and you're just worried that the nutrients have been completely sapped from the compost, you can apply a top dressing of fresh compost. To do this, remove the top 10-12.5cm (4-5in) of compost from the pot and replace it with a new enriched house-plant compost. Repeat yearly to provide the plant with fresh nutrients without disturbing or damaging the roots.

If possible, though, it is always advisable to repot, even if this is potentially a two-person job. Ideally repot in the spring, before the growing season, and avoid repotting if the plant is in flower. The day before, water to slightly dampen the soil, as this will make it easier to remove the plant from its pot on the day.

If there are holes in the bottom of the pot, tip the container gently to one side and poke a garden cane through the holes to loosen the soil from below. Take your time, be patient, eventually you will be able to remove the plant from the pot.

If the plant is sitting directly in a clay or terracotta pot and you are finding it difficult to remove it, try running a knife around the edge of the pot and gently tugging at the stem. Once the plant is out, loosen the compost with your hands and tease out the roots. Remove any excess compost from the root ball as this may contain harmful salts (a build-up of residue from house-plant feed) rather than any nutrients.

The new pot should be 2.5–5cm (1–2in) larger than the original one, any larger and your plant can go into shock. If the new pot does not have a drainage hole, line the bottom with pebbles or chunks of polystyrene to create a false drainage area. Pop a few centimetres/ inch of new house-plant compost in the bottom (sufficient that the plant sits about 2cm/just over ½in below the rim of the pot to allow for watering) and gently place the root ball on top. Add more compost around the roots up to the base of the stem, pressing firmly to stabilise the plant. Give the plant a nice big water and if it is a sun lover, keep out of bright sun for at least two weeks until the plant has settled.

PETS AND PLANTS

As your plants grow, they always seem to become much more alluring to certain pets. For some reason, house plants also present themselves as the perfect snack, despite the fact that some large plants can be seriously toxic to many pets. At the top of each plant entry we identify if it is pet safe.

It is not known why cats and dogs decide to eat house plants. It could be due to a nutrient deficiency that they are trying to remedy or as a cure if they are feeling unwell. One theory is that cats and dogs graze on plants, and especially grass, to calm the stomach.

If you are looking for a large statement plant for your home and you have pets, steer clear of toxic plants such as the Weeping Fig, Devil's Ivy or False Shamrock. Instead, look at completely pet-safe plants such as the Kentia Palm or Spider Plant.

One of the main issues that I have with my dog and house plants is the enjoyment he takes in burying his toys in the compost of our larger plants, especially just after watering. The damp compost seems to be irresistible to him. His pesky paws will often find roots and risk damaging the stability of the plant. To help dissuade your pet from doing this either place a repellant of clove oil-soaked cotton-wool balls under the top layer of compost or pop pine cones on the surface to make the compost less accessible.

BIG PLANTS, BIG PROBLEMS

WITH BIG PLANTS COMES BIG
RESPONSIBILITY — AND SOMETIMES
BIG PROBLEMS.

One of the main issues with big house plants is their weight, which makes it difficult to move them around. A handy piece of kit for moving heavy plants is to make or buy a small plant pot trolley to roll them around your home. A plant trolley is also useful if you need to rotate a plant to ensure even light exposure.

The bigger your plant gets, the more water and nutrients it will need to thrive. Make sure you increase the amount of fertiliser it receives, as failing to do so may cause yellowing of the leaves or leggy growth.

What if your plant is outgrowing your space? If your house plant is getting a bit intrusive, the easy option is to trim back the stems and leaves (ideally do this in spring; avoid when the plant is in flower). I know some people can feel a little guilty at restricting the growth of their plant, but trimming back really won't do any harm and will just give the remaining plant a healthy boost. Alternatively, you may be able to split the plant and repot in separate pots (see Repotting Larger Plants on page 19).

BIG PLANTS

 BIDL

☀ Up to 1m (3ft)

☢ Mildly toxic
Skin irritant

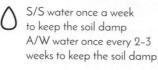 S/S water once a week
to keep the soil damp
A/W water once every 2-3
weeks to keep the soil damp

🧪 S/S feed every 2 months

 Air purifier

〰 Mist occasionally

SPIDERWORT

TRADESCANTIA SPP.

A long and trailing plant that can adapt to almost any conditions, the Spiderwort is the perfect large plant for the smaller home where it will happily sit in a macramé hanging basket or drape from a high shelf or bookcase. One of the prettiest varieties is *Tradescantia zebrina*, which has beautiful striped leaves in green, silver and purple. See the white and green variegated *Tradescantia fluminensis* pictured opposite.

This super fast-growing plant may require moving the pot around a bit to accommodate its exuberance. Fortunately, Spiderwort is very tolerant and will adapt well to bright, indirect light as well as low-light conditions. However, in lower light levels the leaves will lose their variegation and the stems may start to grow quite leggy. To avoid straggly-looking growth, pinch back to a node to encourage a much fuller growth.

The soil should be kept moist and humidity high, which makes the Spiderwort a great plant for the bathroom.

It is easy to propagate by cutting a small piece of stem which has at least one leaf, and planting in free-draining potting compost.

 Sun (not midday)/ BIDL

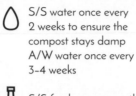 S/S water once every 2 weeks to ensure the compost stays damp A/W water once every 3-4 weeks

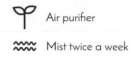 Air purifier

Up to 1.8m (6ft)

Mildly toxic

S/S feed once a month

Mist twice a week

BURMESE FISHTAIL PALM

CARYOTA MITIS

The distinctive feathered and ragged-edged leaves of the Fishtail Palm ensure that as this plant grows in size it will also grow in impact, perfect for filling out a quiet corner in any room. As a member of the palm family, each leaf is produced from a single stem. This is extremely helpful when it comes to propagating as the plant can easily be split and separated into new pots. This is a fast-growing plant, so you will notice the new pots filling up pretty quickly – make sure they have room to grow!

Like most palms, the Fishtail Palm is a sturdy plant that requires very little maintenance. Although it is from the tropics and partial to some bright sun, keep the plant away from the midday sun. The leaves can burn quite easily when exposed to hot sun, leaving a raw brown edge that cannot recover. If browning occurs, cut down any brown leaves so that the plant can put all of its energy into creating new healthy ones. Fishtail Palms love a high humidity, so stand the pot in a bowl of wet pebbles, a centimetre or two inch deep, and as the water evaporates it will increase the humidity around the plant. Keep the compost moist, but not soggy to avoid root rot and ensure that there is ample drainage.

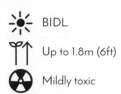 BIDL

Up to 1.8m (6ft)

Mildly toxic

 S/S water 1-2 times a week/
Moist soil
A/W water sparingly

S/S feed every 2 weeks

 Air purifier

Mist weekly
during winter

BIRD OF PARADISE

STRELITZIA REGINAE

Famed for its beautiful orange flowers, the Bird of Paradise is an eye-catcher in any room. It is usually available as quite a big plant to start with and is a fairly slow grower, so you probably won't notice too much growth year on year unless you repot regularly. Repot every two years until the plant is mature, then leave it to get slightly root bound to encourage flowering.

Once repotted, the Bird of Paradise can go on to produce numerous new leaves throughout the growing season. These fresh leaves are prone to shredding and tearing, so place the plant somewhere that it won't get brushed past many times per day.

Typically flowering in late winter to early spring, the Bird of Paradise is shy to bloom in cooler climates, especially for the first year or two. The best position to encourage flowering is bright, indirect light (occasionally direct sunlight). Keep the plant pot bound and regularly feed it. Through the warmer summer months, if you have a garden you can also move the plant outside. Just remember to bring this tender exotic inside before the first frost!

 BIDL

Up to ½m (1.5ft)

Moderately toxic

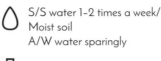 S/S water 1–2 times a week/
Moist soil
A/W water sparingly

 S/S feed weekly

CHINA ROSE

SOLENOSTEMON

The bushy brightly coloured and showy leaves of the China Rose, also known as the Coleus, make it a welcome addition to your house-plant collection, seeing this plant en masse can almost give the visual illusion of flowers while only bearing foliage. The *Solenostemon* is great if you want to fill a large pot or corner spot.

Solenostemons are sub-tropical plants so they will thrive in a humid environment, an ideal spot for them would be in the bathroom. Throughout the spring and summer months when the leaves are full, ensure the compost is moist but well-drained, even just place the pot on a tray of wet pebbles.

When it comes to sun exposure and plants, the narrower the leaves the brighter sun they can endure. They will look their best all year round, but if the leaves become leggy and you would like to encourage bushiness, pinch out the tips in spring and cut back in winter.

 Low light/BIDL

 Up to 1m (3ft)

 Moderately toxic

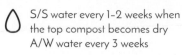 S/S water every 1–2 weeks when the top compost becomes dry
A/W water every 3 weeks

 S/S feed every 2 weeks

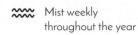 Mist weekly throughout the year

GREEN VELVET ALOCASIA

ALOCASIA MICHOLITZIANA 'FRYDEK'

The arrow-shaped leaves of this *Alocasia* are almost velvet to the touch. This, along with their contrasting, deeply etched white veins and long, arching stems, make it a great addition to any house-plant collection.

The Green Velvet Alocasia should be kept away from any direct sun as the sun will easily scorch the leaves. If a leaf becomes damaged, ideally prune back the whole stem in order to promote healthier growth.

Water freely throughout the summer months as this is when it will be in its peak growing period, and water much less frequently during winter when the plant can be very susceptible to root rot. You may need to support the stem at the base of the plant as it grows to prevent the weight of the sturdy leaves causing the main stem to topple. The Green Velvet Alocasia desires a high humidity, so it is the perfect plant for the bathroom or kitchen.

This *Alocasia* can be propagated via division. A newly purchased plant may have a few stems in each pot, these can be separated out to create more plants or alternatively can be grown all together in one pot with many more to create a much fuller-looking plant.

ANGELA TYE

@GRAENSTUDIOS

Founder of Graen Studios, Angela Tye offers design-led products for the art and practice of growing plants. The name Graen comes from the Icelandic word for green.

My favourite plant is...Prayer Plant *Maranta leuconeura*

The leaves of the Prayer Plant are very striking, with attractive splotches in a range of greens, depending on the variety. This tropical plant likes a high humidity, so it is perfect for a bathroom.

I bought this Prayer Plant in 2017 from a local plant shop when I lived in Copenhagen. Not only is it a beautiful plant, with distinctive splotches on the leaves, but it has an unusual feature – at night the leaves close in an upward position, like praying hands, which is why it's called the Prayer Plant.

I found it grew quite slowly in Denmark, and only really started getting going when my partner and I moved back to England. In fact, it got so large I had to split it into two plants, but I'm planning to move both plants back into one larger pot.

This particular plant's claim to fame is that I took a cutting of it to the first London Terrariums Plant Swap in 2018. This yearly event is a great way to meet fellow plant enthusiasts and come away with some interesting new plants.

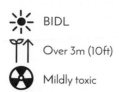 BIDL

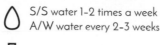 S/S water 1–2 times a week
A/W water every 2–3 weeks

 Air purifier

Over 3m (10ft)

S/S feed once a month

Mist once a week

Mildly toxic

SWISS CHEESE PLANT

MONSTERA DELICIOSA

Perhaps the most-loved of the giants, Swiss Cheese Plants are often seen trailing and climbing across Instagram and Pinterest boards, a favourite due to their huge cut-out leaves and notably easy nature.

As the Cheese Plant grows in size, it will start to shoot out long aerial roots. These long roots at the base of the plant will occasionally stretch outside of the pot; do not cut these, but gently place the tips back in the compost in the pot where they can access water and nutrients.

When Cheese Plants are young and growing rapidly, they will need repotting every year. However, more mature plants will only need to be repotted every two or three years. They are also easy to propagate. Do this either by separating the plant when repotting or by trimming off a stem. To remove a stem, use a clean pair of scissors or gardening snips to cut just below the nearest node, and include any aerial roots if possible. Pop the stem in a cup of water and wait for signs of any small white roots emerging from the brown aerial root. When the white roots are a few centimetres/an inch long, transfer the new plant to a pot filled with potting compost.

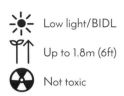

Low light/BIDL

Up to 1.8m (6ft)

Not toxic

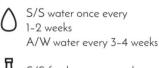

S/S water once every 1–2 weeks
A/W water every 3–4 weeks

S/S feed once a month

Air purifier

Mist every week all year round to prevent browning of the tips

KENTIA PALM

HOWEA FORSTERIANA

Harking back to the glorious palm houses of the Victorian era, the Kentia Palm, also known as the Sentry Palm, is still a firm favourite for conservatories and garden rooms, and you will often see its stems arching and leaves pressing up against many a plant-lover's window. Its popularity is also due to the fact that it is pretty tolerant of almost all conditions, so is very easy to look after.

Kentia Palms prefer bright, indirect light, but will also sit happily in a shady corner of a room. Although Kentia Palms are tolerant of dry air, it is a good idea to mist the leaves regularly to prevent any brown and crispy tips. If you notice any brown or burnt leaf tips, take a pair of scissors and gently trim them off on the diagonal, mimicking the shape of the natural spear leaves.

Bear in mind that the Kentia Palm needs room to grow and spread. Its leaves have the widest span compared to many other popular house-plant palms. Growth is fast for this giant, but don't worry about regular repotting as it struggles with too much root disturbance, so repot only when it has become pot-bound. When repotting, you can also use this as an opportunity to split the plant if it is getting too big for your home.

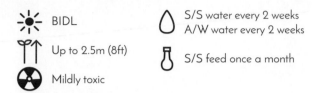

BIDL

Up to 2.5m (8ft)

Mildly toxic

S/S water every 2 weeks
A/W water every 2 weeks

S/S feed once a month

YUCCA

YUCCA GUATAMALENSIS (FORMERLY Y. ELEPHANTIPES)

Tall and striking, the Yucca makes a welcome addition to any house-plant collection. It's a sturdy plant that can adapt to most environments and which you can easily house and watch flourish for many years. The Yucca will grow tall without any need for support, and better still the spiky green leaves crowning the top of the trunk make this a perfect plant for a small space, as the canopy can sweep over a side table or chair without causing too much disturbance.

Place in a bright, sunny room where your Yucca can receive as much bright, indirect sunlight as possible for stronger, greener leaves. The Yucca is quite prone to root rot, so ensure it is planted in a free-draining compost. Misting isn't necessary, but it needs to be watered once every two weeks throughout the year.

Yuccas like to be rootbound, so only repot every two or three years. It is easy to propagate in the autumn from pups that appear at the base of the plant. Select a pup with good green growth and scrape away the soil to expose the roots beneath. Using a clean knife, cut away the pup complete with several centimetres/an inch of root. Plant in succulent potting compost, water and wait!

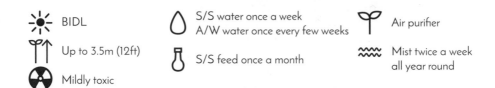

☀ BIDL

🌱⬆ Up to 3.5m (12ft)

☢ Mildly toxic

💧 S/S water once a week
A/W water once every few weeks

🧪 S/S feed once a month

🌱 Air purifier

〰 Mist twice a week
all year round

MINI MONSTERA

RHAPHIDOPHORA TETRASPERMA

The Philodenron Minima, often referred to as the Mini Monstera due to its similarity to the larger, better-known Swiss Cheese Plant is a small plant that will grow and grow fast! For me, this plant actually seems to be a mixture of the Devil's Ivy and Swiss Cheese Plant, a tall, vine-like plant with the distinctive cut leaves of the Monstera that attaches itself to trees and walls for stability.

The Mini Monstera's focus is on growing upwards rather than outwards, so you will not get the width with this plant. It is also one of those plants that as much as the stem grows taller, the leaves will always seem to stay the same size at around 15-20cm (6-8in).

The Mini Monstera will continue to grow taller without much need for repotting. A small pot will suffice for the first few years, although the attractive wavy stem will probably need a plant support such as a bamboo cane, gardening cane or small moss stick with some plant clips. Propagate it in the same way as for the Swiss Cheese Plant (see page 40).

TYLOR ROGERS

@URLOCALPLANTBOY
@ARIUMBOTANICALS

The founder of Arium Botanicals in Portland, Oregon, USA, Tylor Rogers specialises in selling unusual house plants and handmade ceramics.

My favourite plant is...Mini Monstera, *Rhaphidophora tetrasperma*

I was gifted this 18-month-old *Rhaphidophora tetrasperma* (see page 46) from a grower before I moved to Portland in 2017.

This tropical species, part of the Philodendron family, is notorious for not doing anything at first and then absolutely taking off once it gets started. It's been incredibly easy to grow. I water it every seven to ten days and give it nice strong light. So carefree!

While this easy-going plant is one of my favourites, another of my most-loved house plants is much trickier to grow.

Anthurium magnificum x *crystallinum*

A cousin of the Philodendron family, *Anthurium magnificum* x *crystallinum* has large, velvety green leaves with contrasting white veins. This rare jungle plant needs a free-draining soil and a humid environment, such as a bathroom or kitchen.

I picked this hybrid of *Anthurium magnificum* and *crystallinium* while I was working in a plant shop in Chicago. There were only three in stock at the time and I've never seen them anywhere else since!

It's been somewhat of a challenge to grow, and has involved trying different things and figuring out what it wants. I've found high humidity is key for this plant!

BIDL

Up to 60cm (2ft)

Mildly toxic

S/S water once a week
A/W water every 2 weeks

S/S feed every 2 weeks

Air purifier

Mist regularly
throughout the year

PEACE LILY

SPATHIPHYLLUM WALLISII

A relatively simple plant to look after, the Peace Lily is also amazing at purifying the air and is a plant that is often recommended for the bedroom for this reason. The species ranges in size from small varieties that only reach about 38cm (15in) to large, leafy specimens that can grow to 60cm (2ft) or more. When given the right conditions, these elegant plants will produce brilliant white shell-shaped blooms.

While Peace Lilies are happy sitting in low light levels, you will be left with a large leafy friend and no blooms, but it's the flowers that are the real attraction. In order to flower, Peace Lilies need good, bright, indirect light, and even then they can be shy to flower.

Water Peace Lilies so that the soil is moist but not soggy. Allow the top layer of compost to dry out between waterings; ample drainage is very important. However, they are very good at letting you know when they need a top up, as the leaves start to droop and the flower stems arch.

Peace Lilies are propagated by division, which means that they are great for potting multiple plants in one pot to create the illusion of a much fuller plant.

 Sun/BIDL

Up to 90cm (35in)

Mildly toxic

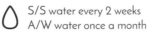 S/S water every 2 weeks
A/W water once a month

S/S feed once a month

 Air purifier

MOTHER-IN-LAW'S TONGUE

SANSEVERIA TRIFASCIATA LAURENTII

We can happily give the Mother-In-Law's Tongue, also known as the Snake Plant, the award for the most low-maintenance of the plants included in this book. With its sturdy, tongue-shaped leaves, this sculptural-looking succulent adds an interesting contrast to most house-plant collections. It is also one of the best plants at purifying the air around you.

Although the Snake Plant will survive well in a shady spot, it will thrive best near a south-facing window with plenty of sun. To help it to get the light it needs, try raising the plant on a plant stand, which will also help to give the illusion of a bigger plant. Because these plants are quite slow-growing, a handy tip to create more of an impact is to place a few plants into one pot. This also means you don't need to repot a Snake Plant often; in fact it likes to become pot-bound before being given a roomier home.

The main problem with the Snake Plant is that its roots can easily rot. Ensure it has a free-draining compost - maybe mix the soil with a few handfuls of horticultural sand or grit to help - and never let the roots stand in water.

 BIDL

Up to 30cm (1ft)

Moderately toxic

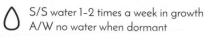 S/S water 1-2 times a week in growth
A/W no water when dormant

 S/S feed every 1-2 weeks in growth

FALSE SHAMROCK

OXALIS TRIANGULARIS

You may not expect to see this dainty plant in a book of big house plants, but given the correct care False Shamrock will grow into a full purple dome. Do not fret when your *Oxalis* dies back during the winter, and definitely do not throw it away, as it will come back in the summer.

Throughout the summer months you will notice a scattering of trumpet-shaped white flowers covering the plant. Each flower will only last a few days at a time before dying back, making room for the next. To encourage new growth, pull out the dead flowers complete with stems; this will also help to keep the plant looking fresh.

Like most bulb-type plants the *Oxalis* will go into dormancy throughout winter, which can be for a period of weeks. Remove the dead leaves and wait for signs of new growth before you start to water again.

False Shamrock rarely needs repotting, even when new growth occurs it will continue to come from the central bulb rather than spreading or sprouting around the pot. However, you can always propagate by removing the bulb from the compost (best to do this towards the end of the dormant period) and breaking apart the bulb offsets to repot.

VICTORIA HELLUM

@PLANT_JOY

Founder of Plant Joy, Victoria Hellum has a background in interior design and runs botanical workshops around the UK.

My favourite plant is...False Shamrock *Oxalis triangularis*

I was gifted my *Oxalis triangularis* (see page 54) five years ago by my mother-in-law in Norway.

I had always admired her *Oxalis*, so she dug up some rhizomes for me to take home. The delicate leaves and stems had all broken during the flight and I was really upset, not realising how hardy they are. I then planted the rhizomes in soil when I got home and crossed my fingers!

Oxalis is not hard to grow, once I understood that it goes into dormancy and comes back to life (it goes dormant quite suddenly towards the end of summer, but this mostly happens only every few years or so, and the plant usually reappears after a few weeks).

At first I thought I'd killed it! *Oxalis* is so easy to propagate that it sometimes happens unintentionally. A case in point is when I break up the rhizomes during repotting (I'm not the best at being meticulous about my soil etc. when potting up). What soil is left on the ground gets swept up and put back in the soil bucket. This means that tiny bits of the rhizomes will end up in my potting mixture and often find their way into other pots. Many of my indoor plants have a 'rogue *Oxalis*' growing with them for company. I gave some plants to my niece and she sent me a message to ask what was going on as an *Oxalis* had sprouted in her *Peperomia*!

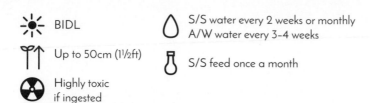

☀ BIDL

⚘ Up to 50cm (1½ft)

☢ Highly toxic
if ingested

💧 S/S water every 2 weeks or monthly
A/W water every 3-4 weeks

⚗ S/S feed once a month

PADDLE PLANT

KALANCHOE THYRSIFLORA

The quiet beauty of this succulent lies in its neatly paired leaves that form a basal rosette and in its subtle leaf colouring – each rounded, fleshy sage-green leaf is covered in a soft white bloom, the tips often tinged with a contrasting red.

Native to South Africa, this succulent will appreciate as much bright light as possible and is even happy basking in a few hours of direct sun on winter days. Rotate the plant regularly to ensure even growth and colouration. Water the plant sparingly and if possible try not to get any water on the leaves as this can cause them to rot. Make sure the compost is free-draining – a mixture of two parts potting compost and one part horticultural sand is ideal – and allow the soil to dry out completely between watering.

This is not a plant that will necessarily grow in height, but the pairs of leaves will continue to grow from the base of a parent set. Repot in spring if the Paddle Plant becomes too crowded, but it does like to be housed in a cosy pot, so don't go up too big a pot size.

- Bright light
- Up to 2.5m (8ft)
- Mildly toxic
  Spines are a skin irritant
- S/S water every 2–3 weeks
  A/W water every 6 weeks
- S/S feed once every 2 months

MONKEY TAIL CACTUS

CLEISTOCACTUS COLADEMONONIS

What an eye-catcher this cactus is, with its long, hairy stems that look exactly like monkeys' tails hanging down! If you're lucky, it will also produce striking red flowers at the tips of the stems. The Monkey Tail Cactus has the potential to grow into a really big plant, up to 1m (3ft) tall and 2.5m (8ft) wide, and will happily hang, divide and drape itself over a bookshelf or from a hanging basket. However, like most cacti, the fine needles are a skin irritant, so keep the plant out of the way of people passing and curious pets. It is sometimes sold under its old Latin name, *Hildewintera colademononis*.

The perfect environment for the Monkey Tail Cactus is in bright light, it can even tolerate a few hours of direct sun, but too little light will cause the stems to become very thin as they stretch to chase the light. You will also notice the tips of the plant will grow towards the light, so placing it in a rotating hanging pot would be ideal.

Water sparingly, every two or three weeks throughout the summer and even less during winter when the cactus will move into dormancy.

 BIDL

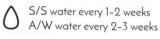 S/S water every 1–2 weeks
A/W water every 2–3 weeks

Mist regularly
all year round

Up to 1m (3ft)

S/S feed every 2 weeks

Not toxic

FISHBONE CACTUS

EPIPHYLLUM ANGULIGER

These strange and fascinating hanging plants are a showstopper at any size. An ornamental cactus, as young plants the flat, zig-zag leaves grow upwards and only with length and maturity will they start to branch down. Fishbone Cacti are best displayed as a hanging plant, either in a sturdy hanging basket or a macramé hanging planter.

Although part of the cactus family, this plant originates from dense and humid rainforests, so the usual cactus care should be disregarded when it comes to watering. Ensure the compost is kept moist throughout most of the year, and during the winter months let the top compost dry out slightly in between watering. The Fishbone Cactus also enjoys a high humidity, out of any direct sun, so regular misting will be highly appreciated. A bright spot in the bathroom where it can enjoy the humidity from daily showers or baths is ideal. If you're not sure your plant is getting enough humidity, look out for aerial roots – this can be a sign that the plant is searching for more water.

If your Fishbone Cactus is starting to look a little thin and leggy, trim back a stem and in its place two more will grow. This is a good technique to encourage a fuller-looking cactus in the same pot.

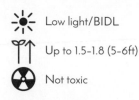 Low light/BIDL

Up to 1.5–1.8 (5–6ft)

Not toxic

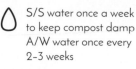 S/S water once a week to keep compost damp A/W water once every 2–3 weeks

S/S feed every 2 months

 Air purifier

Mist once a week all year round

CROCODILE FERN

MICROSORUM MUSIFOLIUM 'CROCODYLLUS'

It is not hard to decipher why this plant is known as the Crocodile Fern. With its wrinkled and scaled leaves, it's not too much a stretch of the imagination to see these resemble the hide of a crocodile. Not necessarily a plant known for its height, the Crocodile Fern shows its majesty in its wide leaf span. Make sure you give this plant plenty of room to spread out, it will look great on a side table or pedestal.

Like most ferns, the Crocodile Fern needs regular watering to ensure the leaves stay green and vibrant. Misting weekly will also help to prevent brown edges on the leaves. Be sure the plant has adequate drainage as Crocodile Ferns are prone to root rot.

The Crocodile Fern has a very shallow root structure and survives without being repotted often. This fern is actually an epiphytic plant, also known as an air plant, which means in its natural habitat it's designed to grow attached to the trunks of trees high up in the forest canopy. This adaptation means that the fern can take most of what it needs from its surrounding environment, capturing water and nutrients from the air. To keep the Crocodile Fern happy, don't let it get too cold, sit it away from draughts and ensure that the air is humid.

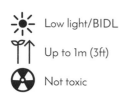 Low light/BIDL

Up to 1m (3ft)

Not toxic

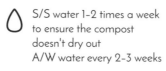 S/S water 1-2 times a week
to ensure the compost
doesn't dry out
A/W water every 2-3 weeks

S/S feed every 2 weeks

 Air purifier

Mist regularly

BOSTON FERN

NEPHROLEPIS EXALTATA 'BOSTONIENSIS'

You will have to be a devoted plant parent in order for your Boston Fern to reach a large and healthy size, mainly through a dedication to providing the right growing conditions. The perfect location for healthy growth is somewhere cool, with low light and high humidity. The Boston Fern suffers terribly from browning of the fronds if the humidity around it is too low, so this is a great plant to have in the bathroom. To appreciate the beauty of its long, sprawling fronds, place it high up on a shelf or in a hanging basket.

To ensure that the compost is kept damp, check the soil every other day if possible. There is an ongoing debate about whether you should mist your Boston Fern too often. Some plant experts argue this may encourage disease that can eventually kill the plant. A better option is to stand the pot on a large tray of wet pebbles, a centimetre or two inch deep, and as the water evaporates it will increase the amount of moisture around the plant. If the leaves start to brown and crisp up, this is a sign that the compost has dried out too much. Unfortunately the leaves will not bounce back, so the best thing to do is trim them right back to the base of the plant to allow the plant's energy to go into producing fresh and healthy new leaves.

JESS SNOWBALL

@JESS.SNOWBALL

Glasshouse horticulturist at The Chelsea Physic Garden in London, Jess Snowball is also a columnist for *Gardens Illustrated*.

My favourite plant is...African Milk Tree
Euphorbia trigona f. rubra

A very easy-care, thorny succulent that has a striking architectural appearance. It's easy to propagate by cuttings (treat it as for Prickly Pear, see page 130). But beware the sap, as it is a skin irritant.

I was given this African Milk Tree as a birthday present some six years ago. It started off about 20cm (8in) tall, and it is now roughly 1.4m (4½ft)! There's no secret to growing this one big, it's so tough.

A good example of the plant's tenacious nature is when I moved from Manchester to London and my mum looked after it for me.

She kept it in her conservatory, where it grew so well. I could only take it back when I moved into a big enough house. Now it's been back in London with me for about a year. However, it hadn't been repotted since a tiny plantlet, so with the help of my boyfriend Tom, we gave it a go, but it was impossible! The Milk Tree seemed to be growing fine, but the rootball had almost suffocated itself. We hacked at the rootball for over an hour to loosen all of the old mix and afterwards there was pretty much nothing left of the roots! We replanted it and it looked absolutely battered and skinny, but now it has started to put out new growth. Yay!

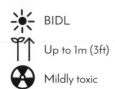

☀ BIDL

⇡ Up to 1m (3ft)

☢ Mildly toxic

💧 S/S water once every week
A/W water every 2–3 weeks

🧴 S/S feed monthly

〰 Mist weekly
throughout the year

WAX FLOWER

HOYA LINEARIS

A new plant on the succulent plant scene, the Wax Flower, also known as the Porcelain Flower, is a hanging beauty that resembles rain with its long, thin leaves trailing down the elegant vines. Its common name comes from the small, white, star-like flowers that look as though they're made of wax.

The Wax Flower is an epiphyte that grows on trees, so as a house plant give it a free-draining substrate.

This plant is used to tropical humid conditions, so it is perfect for a bathroom. Throughout winter you can place it in direct sun for a few hours as too little sun in the darker months can cause the leaves to drop. Do not allow the compost to dry out between watering.

A great plant for a small space, the Wax Flower will grow well, and flower more freely, from a very small pot, where the roots are contained. Each flower should be removed once it has finished blooming. This encourages a new stem to form in its place, ensuring full growth and preventing the plant from becoming bare and leggy.

 BIDL

 Air purifier

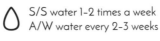 S/S water 1–2 times a week
A/W water every 2–3 weeks

Up to 1.8m (6ft)

Mist once a week

 S/S feed every 2 weeks
A/W feed once a month

Not toxic

SPIDER PLANT

CHLOROPHYTUM COMOSUM 'VITTATUM'

When your spider plant grows at speed and produces thousands of pups, what do you do? Make more Spider Plants! This faithful '70s throwback has gained more and more appeal over the past few years.

Displaying your Spider Plant from a hanging basket is a good way for it to grow to its full potential. Positioned off the floor, the long, thin foliage can grow draping down without resting on the ground. Unfortunately, Spider Plants are prone to developing brown leaf tips. To avoid this, mist regularly and water when the top of the compost has dried out.

Owing to their fast-growing nature, Spider Plants can easily become pot bound. You may have to repot around every other year, using a free-draining compost and ensuring plenty of drainage.

If the conditions are right, during the summer months tiny white flowers will appear on long arching stems from the centre of the plant. From these develop small new plantlets. To propagate, select a plantlet that has developed a cluster of tiny starter roots (nodes) and using a clean pair of scissors cut it from the stem. Insert the baby spider plant into moist potting compost.

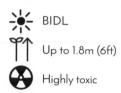 BIDL

Up to 1.8m (6ft)

Highly toxic

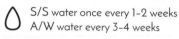 S/S water once every 1-2 weeks
A/W water every 3-4 weeks

 S/S feed once a month

 Mist occasionally
in summer

SAGO PALM

CYCAS REVOLUTA

The appeal of the Sago Palm is its beautiful feathery foliage that fans out from the trunk to form a strong architectural crown. The Sago Palm is not in fact a palm at all, but a member of the Cycad family, an ancient group of forest plants that date back to prehistoric times.

Cycads are shade-loving jungle plants that are found on the forest floor. However, they do appreciate a certain amount of direct sun, especially throughout the cooler winter months. The compost should be kept damp, but ensure it is free-draining and do not let water gather around the crown of the plant as this can cause rotting. Humidity is also key. Place your Palm on a tray of wet pebbles. If the air around the plant is too dry, the leaves will start to brown. Rotate the plant to ensure equal growth.

One thing you will have to offer a mature Sago Palm, though, is space. Their strong rosette of spiky leaves means it isn't the most practical plant to have in a small space. Conversely, you need to be careful not to knock or bend the leaves as it will take a long time for a replacement to grow. Plant up in a sturdy pot and try placing on a side table or plant stand to appreciate the full show of leaves. This is one plant to avoid if you have small children or pets as the leaves are highly poisonous if ingested.

 Sun

Up to 1.8m (6ft)

 Highly toxic
Wear safety glasses
and protective gloves
when trimming the
plant and carefully
dispose of any cuttings

 S/S water every 2 weeks
A/W water every 1–2 months

 S/S feed once a month

PENCIL CACTUS

EUPHORBIA TIRUCALLI

There are many types of *Euphorbia*, but one of the most popular
house-plant forms is the Pencil Cactus, named because of its long,
thin, branching pencil-like stems. Also known as the Firestick Cactus or
Milkbush, this sought-after plant may turn from green to a warm red
colour when placed in the correct conditions.

Although referred to as a cactus, the Pencil Cactus is in fact a succulent.
As these leafless stems grow taller, they can occasionally lean. To provide
discreet support, use thin green garden canes. You should also rotate the
plant occasionally to ensure the stems grow evenly.

Throughout the summer, ensure the compost dries out completely
between watering, and decrease watering throughout winter when
the plant goes into dormancy. This cactus should be potted in a free-
draining succulent soil and planted in an unglazed clay or terracotta
pot, which will help take any excess moisture out of the compost. The
plant produces a sticky white sap when a stem is cut, which is highly
irritant and toxic to both pets and humans.

BIDL

Up to 30cm (1ft)

Not toxic

S/S water once a week
A/W water every few weeks, allowing
the compost to fully dry out inbetween

S/S feed once a month

CHINESE MONEY PLANT

PILEA PEPEROMIOIDES

With its enthusiasm for producing delightful, quirky-looking succulent pups, the Chinese Money Plant, also known as the *Pilea*, is everywhere.

The round pancake leaves and the plant's ability to grow in an almost spherical way makes it a great display specimen. The Chinese Money Plant likes bright, indirect light and as its leaves and stem will grow towards the light, regularly turn the pot once or twice a week. As the plant grows taller, it may need some extra support to ensure it doesn't get too top heavy.

As the stem becomes taller and more woody, some lower leaves may fall off. This may be due to nitrogen deficiency, which affects older leaves first and can be remedied by using a nitrogen-rich plant food.

Repotting and splitting out the pups of this plant is easy to do. It will also encourage the growth of the mother plant by giving her roots more room to manoeuvre. Remove the pups when they are about 5cm (2in) tall. Use a sharp, clean knife to cut the plantlets about 5mm (¼in) under the soil, then place in moist potting compost. You can also leave the pups to develop within the parent pot, for a much fuller looking display.

JEMMA CHARMAN

@GREENROOMS_MARKET

Co-founder of Green Rooms
Market, Jemma Charman has
had a life-long passion for
plants and gardening. Green
Rooms Market organises
regular markets and pop-
up events for independent
sellers of plants and all things
botanical to sell their wares.

My favourite plant is...Chinese Money Plant
Pilea peperomioides

This Chinese Money Plant (see page 78) was given to me two and half years ago as a tiny inch-tall propagated plant from an ex-colleague at a department store, where I was a homeware buyer. It was a leaving present when I left to go on maternity leave.

This plant is special as I feel it is so representative of me and the Green Rooms Market journey. My maternity leave was the real catalyst to starting a botanical market business with my sister Annie, at a time when I was craving more plants in my life.

I found having house plants around me and caring for them a cathartic form of healing from the totally life-altering experience of having a baby.

The Chinese Money Plant is very easy to grow – it's the perfect plant for beginners – and it just keeps on giving. It is a prolific reproducer, and I have lost count of the number of baby plants I have grown from this one and gifted to friends.

 BIDL

Up to 1m (3ft)

Mildly toxic

 S/S water every week to ensure the compost does not dry out
A/W water once every 2-3 weeks

S/S feed every 2 weeks
A/W feed every 6 weeks

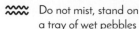 Do not mist, stand on a tray of wet pebbles

TROUT BEGONIA

BEGONIA MACULATA

Another show-stopper of a house plant, the Trout Begonia, also known as Spotted or Polka Dot Begonia, has risen in popularity and demand over the past few years thanks to its spectacularly spotted leaves.

A location with bright but indirect light near a window, away from any draughts is ideal. The leaves are excellent at following the sun, so to encourage even growth you will need to turn the pot regularly.

The compost should be kept damp but not soggy and, unlike a lot of leafy house plants, keep your misters away from this Begonia as water on the leaves can cause scarring and unattractive leaf damage. However, Trout Begonias do like a humid environment, so it's a great idea to stand the pot on a tray of wet pebbles, so that as the water evaporates around the plant, it adds moisture to the air.

To encourage better growth, repot young plants every spring, and once mature every other year. Look out for the plant becoming dormant and its leaves starting to lose colour, signs that the plant is rootbound.

 Bright light

 Up to 3m (10ft)

 Mildly toxic
Skin irritant

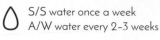 S/S water once a week
A/W water every 2–3 weeks

 S/S feed once a month

 Air purifier

 Mist 2–3 times a
week throughout
the year

WEEPING FIG TREE

FICUS BENJAMINA

As a small plant, the Weeping Fig will quickly take on the appearance of a tiny tree. As it grows into a much larger specimen, the very thin, woody stems arch down in a weeping form, housing tiny, elegant green glossy leaves. This plant hates to be moved, so make sure you find it a spot you're both happy with and keep it there.

Bright light is ideal for the Weeping Fig Tree. It will enjoy a spot that gets the morning sun, but avoid exposure to a hot afternoon sun. You can trim back long and leggy branches to create a fuller-looking tree, but make sure you wear gloves as the cut stems exude a milky sap that's a skin irritant. Regular watering and misting is essential to encourage new growth and to stop leaves from falling, but don't worry if you see some leaf fall during the autumn months, this is natural.

If given the right conditions and repotted regularly, the Weeping Fig Tree can grow quite tall, but you will need the space for such a giant! Carry out repotting every two years during spring, and continue until you are happy with the size of your plant. Once you stop repotting, growth will significantly slow down.

 BIDL

 Up to 1.8m (6ft)

Mildly toxic

 S/S water every 2 weeks
A/W water every 3-4 weeks

S/S once a month

Air purifier

Mist a few times
per week or place
in a bathroom

MING TREE

POLYSCIAS FRUTICOSA 'MING'

Although not the most popular of house plants right now, the Ming Tree, also known as the Ming Aralia, is the perfect plant if you'd like something large in your home but don't actually have much space. The Ming Tree grows tall and compact, rarely reaching out where it isn't wanted. The foliage is fern-like in appearance and looks quite delicate, but the good news is this is a hardy plant that once established doesn't actually need too much looking after. It is slow-growing, but in the right conditions can reach up to 1.8m (6ft) in height.

Place in bright, indirect light and avoid any cold draughts – a corner of a south-facing bathroom would be perfect as it also offers the high humidity the Ming Tree thrives on. Misting frequently will also help to stop the leaves from dropping, but unusually this does not go hand in hand with lots of watering. The compost of the Ming Tree should be kept pretty dry, and watering should only be carried out every few weeks in spring and summer. Make sure there is ample drainage to prevent root rot.

 Low light/mid light

 Up to 1m (3ft)

 Not toxic

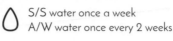 S/S water once a week
A/W water once every 2 weeks

 S/S feed once a month

 Air purifier

 Mist once a week and
keep humidity high

BLUE STAR FERN

PHLEBODIUM AUREUM

This almost alien-looking fern has leaves, or fronds, that are an unusual shade of blue-green and emerge from a central 'furry' brown creeping rhizome. The fronds of this tropical forest epiphyte grow tall and resemble the shape of a rabbit's foot, which explains why it is also known as the Blue Rabbit's Foot Fern.

Bright, indirect light is ideal for strong growth, and this fern can even be kept outside throughout the summer if good weather permits. To encourage a fast and sizeable growth, the Blue Star Fern needs a high humidity, so a position in the bathroom or kitchen will work perfectly. I would also suggest frequent misting to ensure the fronds don't get any browning on the tips.

The Blue Star Fern is another plant that, although it won't necessarily grow huge as a house plant, can be repotted with several plants into one large container to create a luscious sea of blue-green leaves. Propagation is by division and can be done when repotting. Simply separate out the root ball into two parts (or more) and repot the sections into their own pot, ideally using an orchid potting mix.

☀ Sun/BIDL

🌱 Up to 1m (3ft)

☢ Mildly toxic
Skin irritant
Poisonous if ingested

💧 S/S water once a week to
keep the compost damp
A/W water twice a week

🧴 S/S feed every 2 weeks

〜 Mist a few times a week
throughout the year

CROTON

CODIAEUM VARIEGATUM

It is no surprise that the Croton is also known as Joseph's Coat. With its multicoloured, patterned leaves, this is a plant that will undoubtedly stand out against your collection of leafy greens, although it isn't the easiest plant to grow and is known for its fussy nature.

The Croton really doesn't like being moved or repotted, so bear this in mind as the plant matures. Unlike most of the house plants in this book, the Croton will thoroughly enjoy plenty of bright, direct sun. During the hottest summer months, though, check to make sure that the leaves aren't burning in the heat. On the other hand, if it receives too little sun, the bottom leaves may start dropping off. Wipe the leaves with a damp cloth from time to time to keep them dust free.

Throughout the summer, ensure the compost is kept damp. If it dries out too much, you will quickly notice the leaves start to bow down and become flimsy. Over winter, during the plant's dormant period, allow the top few centimetres/inch of soil to dry out before watering. The Croton does love a high humidity, though, so an ideal spot would be a bright bathroom or kitchen. You can also stand the pot on a tray of pebbles, 2.5-4cm (1-1½in) deep, to increase the humidity around the plant.

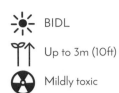 BIDL

Up to 3m (10ft)

Mildly toxic

 S/S water every 2 weeks
A/W water once a month

S/S feed every month

 Air purifier

Mist in winter if using
artificial heating

FIDDLE LEAF FIG

FICUS LYRATA

With its dense woody stem, the Fiddle Leaf Fig isn't the fastest growing plant, but given the right conditions it should be possible to achieve the height and density that you're after.

Fiddle Leaf Figs are generally found as smaller specimens with leaves growing all the way up the stem, very different to the full Fiddle Leaf Fig Trees so often shown on social media. Training your bushy Fiddle Leaf into a tree is relatively straightforward. You will need a plant that is a few years old or about 1.5m (5ft) tall. At this point you may notice that some of the bottom leaves have started to fall off by themselves. If they haven't, carefully remove leaves from the base to form a clear trunk.

To encourage the top of the trunk to branch out, take a sharp scalpel or knife and cut just above a leaf node at a 45-degree angle. Over time (about two or three months) at least one or two new branches will develop at the node, just below the cut. As the plant grows larger, this branching process will start to happen naturally without any help; however the wider your plant gets with extra branches the more chance of it becoming top heavy, so ensure large plants are in stable and heavy pots to support the weight of the branches. Cut back when required.

FANNY ZEDENIUS

@CREATEAHOLIC

It's no secret that bestselling author Fanny has a thing for plants. As a macramé artist, this means her home is filled with lots of beautiful and intricate plant hangers, which allow her to continue to grow her plant gang.

My favourite plant is...Fiddle Leaf Fig *Ficus lyrata*

My Fiddle Leaf Fig (see page 92) is actually two separate plants that I bought on different occasions, I have since planted them in the same large pot to make the plant look fuller.

The first Fiddle Leaf Fig that I bought, Mr. Fiddle, was much taller than the second, Mrs. Fig, for a very long time, and the leaves were considerably bigger. However in the last year or so Mrs. Fig has caught up and is now about the same height. I live in Sweden and I think if the conditions in my home were better suited to Fiddle Leaf Figs, they would be much taller and bigger by now than they are after almost six years.

As I live so far north, they hibernate for most of the year. Once spring and light come they instantly start growing again, but it is such a short season that it takes a lot of time for these two to grow.

Both of my Fiddle Leaf Fig trees have very thin stems. My goal is for them to become large trees and so to achieve this I have implemented a training programme for them! I simulate a pretend jungle storm for a couple of minutes a few times per week, bending them back and forth and in circles. In their natural habitat, Fiddle Leaf Figs sway in the wind and naturally grow thicker stems so as not to break. Hopefully my training programme will give results in the future!

 Sun

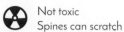 Up to 1.5m (5ft)

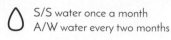 Not toxic
Spines can scratch

 S/S water once a month
A/W water every two months

Spring feed once at the beginning
of the growing season

PERUVIAN OLD MAN CACTUS

ESPOSTOA LANATA

The Peruvian Old Man Cactus, or Cotton Ball Cactus, is covered in a fluffy white coat that makes it clear why this plant has acquired its funny nicknames. The fluff acts as a sunscreen against the scorching sun of its native desert home. Beneath the fluff lies a smothering of sharp spines, so even though this plant looks soft enough to stroke, do not let its woolly coat seduce you!

These cacti grow best when they are exposed to bright sun and should be placed near a window. A south-facing window is fine, but don't expose the plant to direct sun all day as this can cause the cottony white fluff on the cactus to brown and burn. As with most cacti, the Old Man Cactus stores much of its water in its succulent stem, so watering throughout the year can be kept to a minimum. It will thank you for a feed of cactus food in early spring, the start of the growing season. Generally as the Old Man Cactus grows tall, it should also grow in strength, so there should be no need for any plant support. The main thing to remember is to be extremely careful when moving the plant because it can get a little top heavy, and if it is very tall there is the risk of it snapping!

- BIDL
- Up to 7.5m (25ft)
- Mildly toxic
- S/S water once every 2 weeks
  A/W water every 3-4 weeks
- S/S feed once a month
- Air purifier

BENGAL FIG

FICUS BENGHALENSIS 'AUDREY'

This elegant house plant is prized for its large, oval, beautifully veined leaves. The national tree of India, young plantlets are sold as a small bushy plant with leaves growing up the whole length of the woody stem. However, it is possible to trim it into a tree shape by removing the lower leaves. It will grow tall with a rich canopy of leaves that can sweep over furniture.

Like most figs, if the Bengal Fig is exposed to too much direct sun it can cause browning of the leaves, while too little light will cause the leaves to drop. If you have chosen to grow your fig in a tree-like structure, rotate the plant regularly in order to achieve an even growth on all sides. Dust the smooth leaves from time to time to help the plant photosynthesise efficiently, but do not try to remove the thin layer of fuzzy white lines, which are there to protect the plant from any direct sun or heat.

Watering should be carried out regularly. Throughout the summer months, keep the soil damp at all times, but ensure there is adequate drainage as figs are very susceptible to root rot. During the winter, you will need to water less, allow the top few centimetres/inch to dry out between watering.

 BIDL

Up to 1m (3ft)

Not toxic

 S/S water once a week
A/W water every 2 weeks

S/S feed once a month

 Mist throughout the year, if mounted then this can be submerged in water once a week in summer and once every 2 weeks in winter

COMMON STAGHORN FERN

PLATYCERIUM BIFURCATUM

An imposing, almost otherworldly looking plant, the Staghorn Fern can be found in a pot, its antler-like leaves majestically rising from the centre of the plant. Staghorn Ferns are epiphytic, which means in their natural habitat they grow attached to trees and they don't necessarily need to be planted in compost. They have two types of leaves. The first are sterile fronds at the base of the plant whose job is to take up nutrients and water while shielding the roots. Over time, these basal leaves go brown, which is not a sign the plant is dying, but a natural process and they should not be removed. The second type are the distinctive 'antler' fronds, which are spore-bearing fertile fronds that rise from above the roots.

With their delicate and dusty leaves, Staghorn Ferns like bright, indirect light. This 'dust' should be left and not removed as it is there to protect the fronds from excess sun. If you have planted your Staghorn Fern in soil, the compost should be kept damp at all times and the leaves regularly misted. To water board-mounted ferns, submerge the board up to the level of the root ball in a basin or bath of water for about 10 minutes once every few weeks to keep it healthy and the leaves standing strong. Feed it occasionally with a fertiliser suitable for orchids.

BIDL

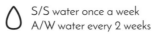 S/S water once a week
A/W water every 2 weeks

 Air purifier

 Up to 3m (10ft)

 S/S feed every 2 weeks

☢ Mildly toxic
Contact with sap can
cause skin irritation

RUBBER PLANT

FICUS ELASTICA

The Rubber Plant can be a little hard to get going from a pup, and the plant needs ample light to avoid leaf drop, but once established there is no stopping this statuesque plant!

Rubber Plants are thirsty, so water thoroughly once a week throughout the summer, ensuring the compost is soaked through. Make sure there is ample drainage as the roots do not enjoy sitting in water and they are quickly prone to root rot. Regularly wipe the leaves with a damp cloth to keep them looking shiny, and make sure they receive the maximum amount of light each day for a happier and healthier plant. Rotate the plant about once a month to ensure even growth.

Like the Fiddle Leaf Fig, it is possible to train the Rubber Plant into a tree-like specimen. Undertake any extensive pruning in spring and early summer to encourage new growth. When pruning a Rubber Plant, watch out for the sticky white sap that seeps from cuts. It is a skin irritant, so wearing gloves is advisable. When the Rubber Plant reaches the desired height, prune the top leaves to prevent any new vertical growth and encourage horizontal leaves to develop, making the plant fuller.

 Low light/BIDL

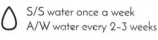 S/S water once a week
A/W water every 2-3 weeks

 Air purifier

Up to 90cm (35in)

 S/S feed once a month

Mist once a week
all year round

Not toxic

CAST IRON PLANT

ASPIDISTRA ELATIOR

The Cast Iron Plant has been wildly popular since the 1970s, partly because of its tolerance to neglect, and also for its potential to outlive most house plants and grow to a full and impressive leafy structure. The long, spear-like leaves will grow directly upwards, not taking up too much space as a young plant, then begin to widen and fill the pot as the plant matures.

Although happy in most light conditions, you should keep the Cast Iron Plant away from the midday sun as this will burn the tips of the leaves, detracting from their rich green colour. Make sure you regularly wipe the leaves to keep them free from any dust and dirt.

Repot young plants yearly in spring, but leave mature specimens in their current pots as long as possible. The Cast Iron Plant hates being disturbed, so repotting once every three years or so is preferable. Ideally propagate by division when you are repotting. To do this, remove the plant from the pot and carefully separate the rhizomes into a clump that has two or three leaves attached. To create a fuller effect in the new planting, add several divisions to the same pot. They will eventually grow together to form a substantial-looking planting.

BIDL

 S/S water twice a week
A/W water once a week

 Mist regularly
throughout the year

 Up to 90cm (35in)

 S/S feed every 2 weeks
A/W feed once a month

 Mildly toxic
Contact can cause
skin irritation

ELEPHANT'S EAR

ALOCASIA ZEBRINA

The talking point of this *Alocasia* lies in its striking zebra-like striped pattern along the long, arching stems. Make the most of this feature by mounting the pot on a low pedestal so that the stems are almost at eye level. The upright, rich-green, arrow-shaped leaves are an added bonus and the perfect foil to the stems.

The Elephant's Ear is a jungle plant that thrives in bright, indirect light. You will need to rotate the plant from time to time to ensure even growth. Not surprisingly, it also likes high humidity. Bear this in mind when finding a location for it in the home, and if you have the space, place it in the bathroom where it can enjoy the steamy conditions. However, it can grow to quite a span, so make sure the plant is out of the way of traffic and there is no chance of leaf damage. Alternatively, place the pot on a tray of wet pebbles, 2.5-4cm (1-1½in) deep, for a boost of humidity. Water regularly throughout the summer months, ensuring the compost is kept damp and that the pot has ample drainage. During winter, decrease watering, but do make sure it has some winter sun.

 Low indirect light/ BIDL

 S/S water every 2 weeks A/W water every 3-4 weeks

 Air purifier

 Up to 1m (3ft)

S/S feed once a month

Mist regularly

 Moderately toxic Skin irritant

COMMON IVY

HEDERA HELIX

The Common Ivy is a perfect decorative plant for inside or outside, it works in almost every situation, from cascading out of an indoor hanging basket to draping itself over a garden wall. There are many varieties available, including variegated types and forms with interesting leaf shapes, a rewarding family that will add pretty greenery to almost any spot in the home. See the *Hedera helix* wonder opposite.

Keep Common Ivy out of direct sun as this may cause the leaves to brown and crisp, but too little light and the ivy will become long and leggy. If the stems start looking quite bare, trim them back to create a fuller-bodied plant that will start to grow new, healthier leaves.

Common Ivy needs good drainage, and if overwatered is quite prone to root rot. If displaying in a hanging basket, ensure compost is free draining and you can always pop the plant in a plastic pot inside the hanging basket to allow water to drain without going all over the floor.

Common Ivy is easy to train to grow around shapes, such as frames in the form of circles or hearts. Simply take trails of ivy and wind them around the frame for instant effect.

BIDL

Up to 1m (3ft)

Mildly toxic

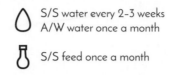

S/S water every 2-3 weeks
A/W water once a month

S/S feed once a month

JADE PLANT

CRASSULA OVATA

You will find a Jade Plant, or Money Tree, in most plant-loving homes, whether as a small succulent in a window pot or as a much larger, mature plant that is starting to resemble a miniature tree.

The Jade Plant is a relatively easy succulent to keep alive. Place it in bright, indirect light for most of the year, but in the cooler winter months a few hours a day of direct sun will be appreciated to stop any leaf dropping.

As the Jade Plant matures, you may need to support the heavy stems with some garden canes. Use garden twine to tie the stems loosely to the cane so that the plant can grow tall and strong.

Jade Plants are easy to propagate from stem cuttings. Using a clean pair of scissors or snips, cut a piece of stem above a node, at least 5-7.5cm (2-3in) long. Remove any sets of leaves towards the bottom of the stem. Set the cutting on one side for a day or two to form a callous before planting it in a soil suitable for succulents. Only water the soil once roots emerge, in about two weeks' time. Once mature, rotate the Jade Plant once a year for equal, round growth.

ANDERS RØYNEBERG

@ARCTICGARDENER

Psychotherapist Anders Røyneberg is a well-known house-plant enthusiast and author based in Oslo, Norway.

My favourite plant is...Calamondin Tree
Citrus x microcarpa (sometimes listed as Citrus mitis)

The Calamondin Tree is a hardy citrus tree bearing small, bitter fruit, similar to a lemon or lime. Although they can be grown indoors, in a bright, sunny room, Calamondins benefit from being placed outside during the warm summer months. The plant is mildly toxic to cats and dogs, but not to humans.

My Calamondin was a gift from a friend in 2009. It was a small house plant then, but now it's taller than me and I am 1.9m (6ft 2in)! I find the Calamondin is quite easy to grow, but as mine grew bigger it became too large for my apartment. Now I move it out onto my balcony during the summer season, and every winter I store it up in the attic where it's cold but

frost-free. I keep it there during the coolest months until the spring light returns, and then I bring it out on my balcony again. I hope it will reach 100 years.

Calamondin is a great citrus type for colder countries such as Norway. The Calamondin is native to the Philippines, a cross between a kumquat (*Citrus japonica*) and a mandarin orange (*Citrus reticulata*), but is hardy and easy-care, even in the northern hemisphere. It produces small fruits about the size of a golf ball during winter and this year I counted 300 tiny citruses! They taste a bit on the sour side, but when sliced are perfect in my weekend libation, G&T.

 BIDL

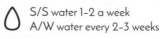 S/S water 1-2 a week
A/W water every 2-3 weeks

 Air purifier

Up to 2.5m (8ft)

S/S feed once a month

Mild to
moderately toxic

DEVIL'S IVY

EPIPREMNUM AUREUM

Called Devil's Ivy for a reason, this plant is almost impossible to kill! It is also sometimes referred to as a Pothos, which is the genera name for this family of tropical climbing vines. Devil's Ivy grows at quite a rapid rate, and is perfect for training up a moss stick, trailing from a hanging basket or spilling from a pot over a bookcase.

This plant will grow more enthusiastically the more light it receives. A lack of light will also cause any leaf variegation to fade, so a bright, sunny spot will provide the perfect conditions for this exuberant grower.

It is very tolerant of neglect in terms of watering, and if the leaves wilt due to insufficient watering, no need to panic. As soon as the roots start to take in moisture, the leaves will bounce right back.

You will quite often see the Devil's Ivy for sale in a small hanging pot, and you will usually be able to keep the plant in this pot for at least another year after purchase before potting on, even if the vines seem to be getting very long.

 BIDL

Up to 2.5m (8ft)

Mildly toxic

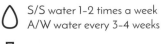 S/S water 1-2 times a week
A/W water every 3-4 weeks

 S/S feed once a month

 Air purifier

Mist regularly
weekly

DWARF UMBRELLA TREE

SCHEFFLERA ARBORICOLA

A fast-growing but adaptable plant for ease of care, the Dwarf Umbrella Plant, also known as the Gold Capella, can tolerate quite a bit of neglect. A bonus is that it is very efficient at cleaning the surrounding air.

The Dwarf Umbrella Plant does well in bright, indirect light, but will be happy enough in a shady spot. However, if it is kept in too dark a space, the plant will tend to grow tall and leggy with thinning out of the attractive umbrella-like leaves. The leaves will grow towards the light, so it's a good idea to rotate the plant pot once a month during the growing period, in order to encourage an equal and rounded growth.

Water the plant regularly when the compost has dried out. The Dwarf Umbrella Plant enjoys a moist compost but not sitting in wet. Allow free draining, and regularly mist to avoid browning of the leaf edges.

Dwarf Umbrella Plants can grow tall and regal, but a moss stick with some plant clips will be very handy for some extra help and to keep them straight.

 BIDL

Up to 1.8m (6ft)

Moderately toxic

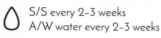 S/S every 2–3 weeks
A/W water every 2–3 weeks

S/S feed once a month

 Air purifier

DUMB CANE

DIEFFENBACHIA AMOENA

The amazing, almost camouflage-like patterns seen on the leaves of the Dumb Cane Plant are their most spectacular when seen en masse, and you will quite often see collections of *Dieffenbachia* grouped together in one long or large pot, giving a lush tropical look for smaller spaces. The leaves originate from one central stem, arching outwards to give a luxuriant, full covering.

The Dumb Cane will grow best and quickest in bright, indirect light – too little light and you will notice the patterns start to fade and the leaves slightly droop. As soon as the plant is placed in brighter conditions, the leaves will bounce straight back. Watering should be slight, ensuring the top of the compost dries out between waterings. You should also rotate the plant to ensure equal growth of leaves around the central stem.

Be aware that the sap of the plant is particularly toxic. The nickname 'Dumb Cane' refers to the fact that if sap is ingested it can cause a painful burning sensation to the mouth and throat, preventing speech. If the sap comes into contact with the skin, it can cause burning and itching. Not a great plant to have around pets or small children.

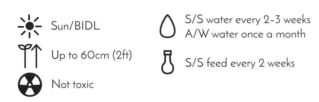

Sun/BIDL

Up to 60cm (2ft)

Not toxic

S/S water every 2–3 weeks
A/W water once a month

S/S feed every 2 weeks

STRING OF HEARTS

CEROPEGIA WOODII

A popular house plant thanks to its cascade of dainty heart-shaped leaves, String of Hearts is a semi-succulent and part of the cactus family. It needs to be housed on a high shelf or in a hanging basket as this hardy plant has the potential to grow fast and long!

A healthy String of Hearts should have firm and full leaves. If the leaves start to feel a little papery-thin, then it's time to give the plant a water. Do not overwater as the roots are prone to rot. However, as the vines grow longer water the plant slightly more to ensure the ends don't become frail and wiry. Like your own hair, every now and again your String of Hearts may need a trim to tidy up any straggly ends!

String of Hearts thrives in a bright room with plenty of sun, while insufficient light may cause the vine to become quite leggy, with large distances forming between each leaf. If the plant is receiving the right amount of sun during the summer, you will be lucky enough to see the small white tubular flowers dotted up and down the stems.

If your String of Hearts has a good length but is looking a bit on the sparse side, add a cutting to the pot to create a fuller-looking plant.

JOE EARLEY

@SOILANDSOLDER

Founder of Soil and Solder, Joe Earley is based in Rochester, Kent, where he handcrafts terrariums to his own designs from recycled glass.

My favourite plant is...String of Hearts *Ceropegia woodii*

I bought my String of Hearts (see page 121) in 2016 from Spiderplant, a great house-plant shop in Brighton that specialises in more uncommon house plants as well as unusual varieties of popular species. As String of Hearts is a succulent, I've found the following 5,1,1 soil mix a great medium for the plant: sphagnum moss (from sustainable sources), perlite, and a tiny bit of soil combined with orchid bark.

The hardest part of caring for a String of Hearts is dealing with the vines, because they tangle so easily. I tried to split the plant into two pots, but they found themselves entwined once again. I've tried to untangle it about 50 times but given up, it just doesn't stop growing!

 Low light/BIDL

 Up to 1m (3ft)

 Mildly toxic
Skin irritant

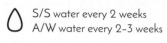 S/S water every 2 weeks
A/W water every 2-3 weeks

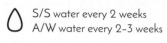 S/S feed once a month

 Air purifier

ZZ PLANT

ZAMIOCULCAS ZAMIIFOLIA

One of the hardiest house plants out there, the ZZ Plant has been a firm favourite since the 1970s. There is little you can do wrong with the ZZ Plant. It survives well in low light, but equally will thrive in a brighter, sunnier spot (but avoid direct sunlight).

You will often find the ZZ Plant in garden centres and plant shops looking as though it's about to burst from its plastic pot, thanks to its large underground rhizomes that are used to store water. Many times I have seen the ZZ plant actually breaking open its container! Because the roots are so efficient at storing water, you should allow the compost to dry out between watering. Overwatering can easily cause root rot.

The stems housing the glossy, waxy leaves shoot directly upwards and rarely branch out, so this is a great plant if you are living in a smaller space, perfect for squeezing next to a sofa or framing a window. Wear gloves when trimming or pruning your ZZ Plant as broken leaves exude a sap that can cause mild skin irritation.

Moderate to low light

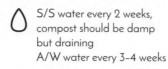 S/S water every 2 weeks, compost should be damp but draining
A/W water every 3-4 weeks

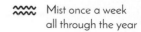 Mist once a week all through the year

 Up to 60cm (2ft)

 Not toxic

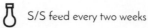 S/S feed every two weeks

CALATHEA SPP.

CALATHEA WARSCEWICZII

There are so many different types of Calathea, each with their own beautiful and distinctive leaf patterns. The leaf markings are often so painterly that a collection of Calathea grouped in a corner can look like a work of art. Although they are all different, most Calathea need the same care, and despite the fact that they can be a tricky species to grow, if you persevere you will eventually get a large, full, leafy plant.

Calathea are tropical jungle plants, so bear this in mind when choosing a location in the home. They love a humid environment and are the perfect plant for a bathroom where they will thrive in the steamy conditions. You can also place the pot on a large tray of wet pebbles, to increase the moist air around the plant. Calathea are also very adverse to draughts, so keep them away from doorways or open windows as chilly breezes may cause the leaves to wrinkle and curl. Even new leaves can occasionally start to open already brown if they get too cold.

Calathea don't need repotting often, once every two years is about right if the roots have filled the pot. They are easily propagated by division.

Sun (not midday)/
BIDL

 S/S water once or twice a week
A/W water once every 2-3 weeks

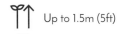 Up to 1.5m (5ft)

S/S feed once a month during
growing season

Moderately toxic

DWARF ELEPHANT'S EAR

ALOCASIA GAGEANA

Perhaps one of the largest plants to have in your home and certainly not
one for a small space, the *Alocasia gageana* is also known as Elephant's
Ear thanks to its show-stopping leaves. These huge, delicate and papery
leaves are upwardly ribbed and have an attractive wavy edge - much
like an elephant's ear. These can be easily broken and damaged, so be
sure to place your giant *Alocasia* where it won't be brushed past as there
is nothing worse than hearing the sound of a leaf being torn.

Rotate the Elephant's Ear occasionally to ensure even growth (as it's
tricky to move, try using a low, rolling plant stand that you can move
around when needed). If you notice any dust on the leaves, use a damp
cloth to remove it. As a big tropical plant, the Elephant's Ear will be
thirsty throughout the summer months, so water plentifully, making sure
the compost stays moist but not waterlogged at all times. Decrease
watering in the winter. It likes a humid environment, so ideally stand the
plant container on a tray of wet pebbles, to provide a moist atmosphere.

Owing to its size, the Elephant's Ear can be a bit of a nightmare to
repot and repotting should be carried out with help. After the plant has
been repotted you will need to make sure the stem is stable.

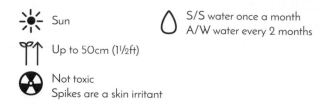

Sun

Up to 50cm (1½ft)

S/S water once a month
A/W water every 2 months

Not toxic
Spikes are a skin irritant

PRICKLY PEAR

OPUNTIA HUMIFASA

Known for their flat, paddle-shaped stems that build up and branch off each other, the Prickly Pear family is a fun desert cacti to have in the home. They do not necessarily need much space when they are young and are pretty slow-growing, but as mature plants you will have to find a space for them away from any contact as their spines can cause mild irritation if touched or brushed against.

As a desert plant, the Prickly Pear craves lots of direct sun – too little will stunt their growth. Watering should be kept to a minimum, as the fleshy pads retain enough water to get them through the dormant growing months.

Opuntia are also quite sensitive to being rootbound. If you notice that you have not had much growth during the summer seasons, then it may be time to go up a pot size. Do this in the summer. Select a pot with drainage holes and, wearing a pair of gloves to protect you from the spikes, place the root ball in a sandy cacti and succulent compost. Make sure when planted that it is not top heavy as cacti are known to have quite small root balls and can easily topple over as they grow.

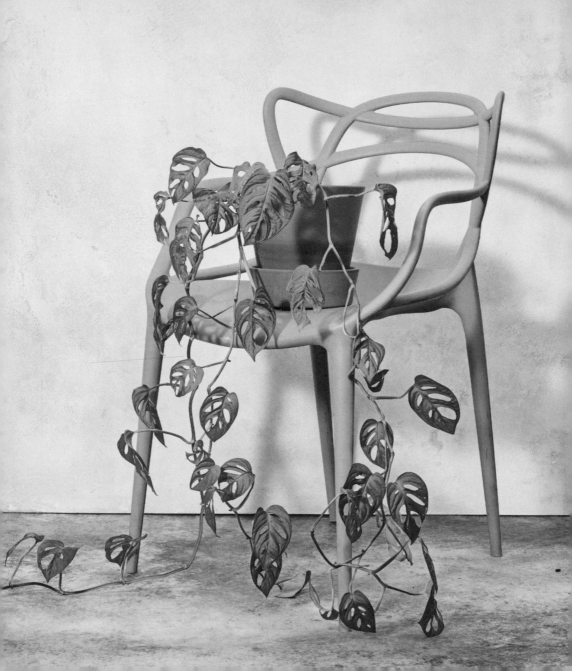

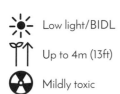 Low light/BIDL

 Up to 4m (13ft)

 Mildly toxic

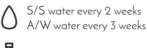 S/S water every 2 weeks
A/W water every 3 weeks

 S/S feed once a month

 Air purifier

 Mist once a week
throughout the year

MONSTERA MONKEY MASK

MONSTERA ADANSONII

One of my all-time favourite plants, this relative of the larger *Monstera deliciosa* is often found for sale as a much smaller plant, but one that has the ability to grow and trail with its beautifully intricate vines. As the leaves of the Monkey Mask don't increase in size as the plant matures, staying at around 10-15cm (4-6in) in length, this makes it much easier to train the vines either to climb up a moss stick from a pot or to hang down from a basket or shelf.

This jungle vine is found in its native habitat hanging from the branches of other trees, so the Monkey Mask is partial to bright, indirect light. However, if it receives too little light, the leaves may start to shrivel and new leaves will not open fully. If this starts to happen, move the pot to a brighter location. Rotate it occasionally to ensure even growth.

Although quite forgiving of neglect, the Monkey Mask should ideally be watered enough to ensure that the compost does not dry out. If the compost dries out too much, you will notice the vines lose their bounce and the leaves start to droop. The good news is that as soon as you water it again you will start to see it springing back to life. Wipe the leaves with a damp cloth occasionally to remove dust and dirt.

 Dappled shade/ BIDL

 Up to 2.5m (8ft)

 Mildly toxic

 S/S water once a week A/W water once every 2-3 weeks

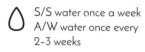 S/S feed once a month

 Mist daily

ASPARAGUS FERN

ASPARAGUS SETACEUS

Neither part of the Asparagus family nor an actual fern (it's technically part of the lily family), *Asparagus setaceus* is often found as a small house plant in garden centres, but be aware, this beauty has the ability to climb and wind itself around your home.

The Asparagus Fern will thrive in dappled shade, but can also adapt to grow in brighter conditions. It loves a humid environment, and will thank you for placing it in a steamy bathroom. It is easy to keep hydrated, just ensure the plant has a free-draining compost and mist regularly. Browning of the lower leaves is a sign that you may need to increase the humidity around the plant. Even if it gets to the stage of looking completely brown and dead, if you trim the plant back completely and continue to water and mist it, the plant should revive quickly.

Despite the fern's soft, light and feathery appearance, as the plant grows in size the stems will start to produce sharp little hooks that they use to latch themselves onto different surfaces or plants. These tiny thorns can be vicious! Wear gardening gloves when pruning an older plant. If content in its environment, the plant may flower and produce small berries. Plant the berries to propagate the fern.

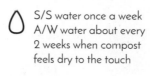

BIDL

Up to 1.8m (6ft)

Not toxic

S/S water once a week
A/W water about every
2 weeks when compost
feels dry to the touch

S/S feed monthly
A/W feed every 2 months

Air purifier

Mist regularly

MONEY TREE

PACHIRA AQUATICA

These beautiful plants are often seen with their stems braided together.
This procedure is carried out when the plants are young and amazingly
as the plant grows, the stems continue to grow in this formation of their
own accord.

Growing best in bright, indirect sunlight, the Money Tree, also known as
Malabar Chestnut, can tolerate a small amount of direct sun, but too
much may burn the leaves. Too little light will cause the leaves to yellow.
Rotate the plant occasionally so that that it doesn't grow lopsided. Water
regularly and do not allow the compost to completely dry out. Money
Trees are thirsty plants, but do ensure they have plenty of drainage to
prevent root rot.

If a Money Tree is young and hasn't yet been braided, it is possible to
do this at home. Pot three small stems together and ensure that they are
flexible enough to plait. Gently move the stems around each other and
if you are having difficulty braiding the entire length of the stems in one
go, release-tie some twine to keep the stems to where you got to, wait
until the plant relaxes some more and try again.

INDEX

Aerial root: A root that grows out from the stem above ground level.

Air purifier: A plant that can absorb harmful toxins from the air.

Epiphytic: An organism that grows on the surface of a plant.

Frond: A leaf of a fern or palm.

Hardy: A plant that can withstand adverse growing conditions, tolerating cold, heat, drought, flooding or draughts.

Humidity: A measure of the amount of water vapour in the air. Plants that originated from a jungle environment like to live in a humid atmosphere.

Leaf node: A small swelling that occurs on a plant stem from which one or more leaves emerge.

Leggy: A plant that has long, spindly, often leafless stems.

Offset: A young plantlet that appears on a mature plant. These can usually be carefully detached and used for propagation.

Plantlets: Young or small plants that grow off of a parent plant, which can be propagated.

Propagation: To breed specimens of a plant by natural processes from the parent stock.

Pup: A plant that develops as an offset from a parent plant.

Root-bound: The roots of a plant that has outgrown its pot and will grow in circles, becoming cramped and tangled.

Substrate: The base on which an organism lives, soil is the substrate of most plants.

Variegated leaves: A rare leaf which has both green and non-green parts.

SUPPLIERS

Whether you are shopping for plants or equipment you'll find everything you need from the shops listed here - these are just some of my favourites.

CONSERVATORY ARCHIVES
A London mecca for all plant collectors.
www.conservatoryarchives.co.uk

LONDON TERRARIUMS
A curated selection of beautifully designed plants and accessories.
londonterrariums.com

WEST ELM
Modern furniture and home decor.
westelm.co.uk

GRAEN STUDIOS
Design-led products for horticulture.
www.graenstudios.com

CREATEAHOLIC
Handmade macramé decor.
createaholic.se

ARIUM BOTANICALS
A Portland-based plant shop selling both plants and accessories.
www.ariumbotanicals.com

THE CHELSEA PHYSIC GARDEN
London's oldest botanical garden with café and gift shop.
www.chelseaphysicgarden.co.uk

GREEN ROOMS MARKET
Organises markets and pop-up events for independent sellers of plants.
www.greenroomsmarket.com

POT PARTY
A fun collection of delightful planters.
www.potparty.co.uk

LAZY GLAZE – HARRIET LEVY-COOPER
Functional ceramics for everyday life.
www.lazyglaze.co.uk

LOUISE MADZIA
A chic collection of quirky planters.
www.louisemadzia.com

SMUG
Independent homewares shop.
www.lizzieforsmug.com

FOREST
Plant and products that bring nature into your home.
forest.london

POTTERY BARN
Stylist home furnishing store.
www.potterybarn.com

LONDON TERRARIUMS

londonterrariums.com

ABOUT THE AUTHOR

Emma Sibley has had a keen interest in horticulture from a young age and after studying Surface Design at university, she changed career direction to work with plants. She took a number of short courses to increase her knowledge and love of all things green. Emma now runs a growing start-up business called London Terrariums and offers workshops, interior displays and private commissions. Emma is a member of the British Cactus and Succulent Society.

ACKNOWLEDGEMENTS

Massive thank you to everyone who has helped to create this third little book: Harriet, Nikki, Stacey and Adam for spending the hottest day of the year shooting and hoisting these giant plants around east London and for generally making this book happen. Thank you to friends who generously loaned out your plants and to Joe, Angela, Jemma, Victoria, Jess, Tylor, Fanny and Anders for sharing your wonderful plant stories with us. And lastly to Walnut Wiggins for striking such a great pose for his pets and plants section!

PUBLISHING DIRECTOR Sarah Lavelle
COMMISSIONING EDITOR Harriet Butt
ASSISTANT EDITOR Stacey Cleworth
SERIES DESIGNER Gemma Hayden
DESIGN AND ART DIRECTION Nikki Ellis and Katherine Keeble
PHOTOGRAPHER Adam Laycock
PROPS STYLIST Faye Wears
ILLUSTRATOR Rachel Victoria Hillis
DOG MODEL Walnut Wiggins
HEAD OF PRODUCTION Stephen Lang
PRODUCTION CONTROLLER Katie Jarvis

Published in 2020 by Quadrille,
an imprint of Hardie Grant Publishing

Quadrille
52-54 Southwark Street
London SE1 1UN
quadrille.com

Cataloguing in Publication Data: a catalogue record for this book
is available from the British Library.

Text © Emma Sibley 2020
Design, layout, illustrations and photography © Quadrille 2020

ISBN 978 1 78713 506 2

Reprinted in 2020
10 9 8 7 6 5 4 3 2

Printed in China

FSC
www.fsc.org
MIX
Paper from
responsible sources
FSC® C020056